READING POWER

High-Tech Vehicles

Aircraft Carriers

William Amato

The Rosen Publishing Group's
PowerKids Press™
New York

Published in 2002 by The Rosen Publishing Group, Inc.
29 East 21st Street, New York, NY 10010

First Edition

Book Design: Christopher Logan

Photo Credits: Cover, pp. 4–5, 10, 12–13, 18–19 © DVIC March Air Force Base, CA; pp. 6–7, 9 (inset), 11 (a, b), 15 (inset) © U.S. Navy photo; pp. 8–9 © George Hall/Corbis; pp. 11 (c), 14–15 © David & Peter Turnley/Corbis; pp. 16–17 © Yogi, Inc./Corbis; p. 21 © Douglas Peebles/Corbis

Amato, William.
Aircraft carriers / William Amato.
    p. cm. — (High-tech vehicles)
Includes bibliographical references and index.
ISBN 0-8239-6012-9 (library binding)
1. Aircraft carriers—United States—Juvenile literature. [1. Aircraft carriers.] I. Title.
V874.3 .A43 2001
623.8'255—dc21
                                        2001000270

Manufactured in the United States of America

Contents

Aircraft Carriers

An aircraft carrier is a ship that takes fighter jets all over the world. The jets take off and land on the deck of the aircraft carrier.

IT'S A FACT!

The U.S. Navy's Nimitz class carrier is the largest type of aircraft carrier. It is more than 1,000 feet long!

An aircraft carrier has a large engine room. The engines make the power that runs the aircraft carrier.

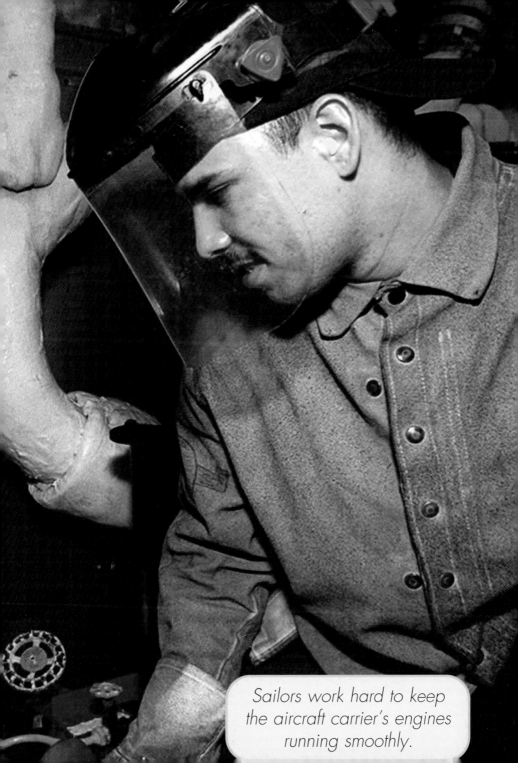

Sailors work hard to keep the aircraft carrier's engines running smoothly.

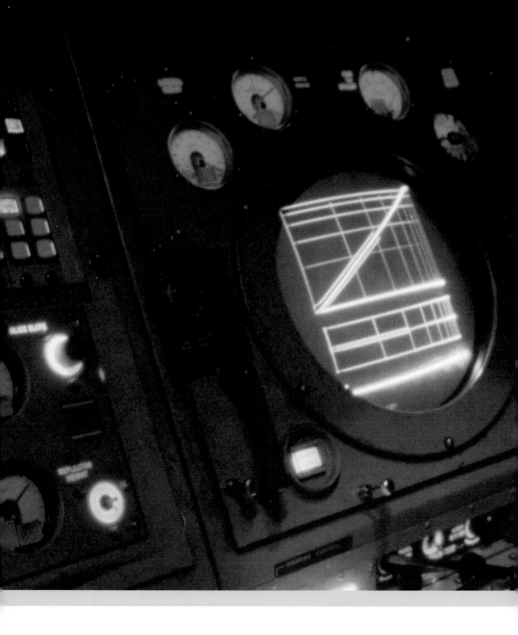

An aircraft carrier has many
computers. The crew uses computers
to help run the carrier. The crew also

These sailors are checking the radar screen.

Radar tells the crew when there are other ships or planes close by.

The Crew

More than 5,000 people live and work on an aircraft carrier. There are many jobs to do.

IT'S A FACT!

The flight deck crew uses hand signals to help the pilots take off and land.

Flight deck crew member

200

10

Repair workers keep the computers and other machines running smoothly. Pilots fly the planes.

Repair workers

Pilots

City at Sea

An aircraft carrier is like a small city. It even has its own post office and fire department.

Taking Care of Business on a Nimitz Class Carrier

Amount of Mail Delivered Each Year	*1,000,000 or more pounds*
Amount of Fresh Water Made Each Day	*400,000 or more gallons*
Meals Served Each Day	*18,000–20,000*
Haircuts Given Each Week	*1,500 or more*
Number of Doctors	6
Number of Dentists	5

This jet is taking off from the deck of an aircraft carrier.

Airport at Sea

Jets use the deck as a runway. Jets have to take off quickly because the runway is very short.

14

The air boss is the person in charge of planes taking off and landing. The air boss works in the air traffic control room.

Jets come back to the carrier when their jobs are done. To land, a jet lowers a hook that catches a cable.

The cable brings the jet to a stop
very quickly.

The airplane hangar deck is below the flight deck.

Giant elevators bring the planes down to the hangar deck. There, work is done on the planes.

An elevator takes this fighter jet down to the hangar deck.

Protecting the World

Aircraft carriers are the biggest ships in the Navy. They are always ready for action.

Seven Types of Aircraft Found on a Carrier

- A-6 *Intruder*
- F-14 *Tomcat*
- S-3B *Viking*
- EA-6B *Prowler*
- F-18 *Hornet*
- E2C *Hawkeye* (helicopter)
- SH-60 *Seahawk* (helicopter)

Nimitz class carriers can hold about 85 planes and helicopters.

Glossary

air boss (air baws) the person in charge of all plane movements on and around the carrier

crew (kroo) a group of people who work together on a ship

flight deck (flyt dehk) the top level of a carrier where planes take off and land

hangar deck (hang-uhr dehk) a place where planes are kept and fixed

radar (ray-dar) an electronic machine that tells the crew when there are other ships and planes close by

runway (ruhn-way) a place where airplanes take off and land

Resources

Books

Supercarriers
by Michael Burgan
Capstone Press (2001)

Aircraft Carriers
by Michael Green
Capstone Press (1997)

Web Site

The United States Navy
http://www.chinfo.navy.mil/navpalib/
   ships/carriers/

Index

Word Count: 258

Note to Librarians, Teachers, and Parents

If reading is a challenge, Reading Power is a solution! Reading Power is perfect for readers who want high-interest subject matter at an accessible reading level. These fact-filled, photo-illustrated books are designed for readers who want straightforward vocabulary, engaging topics, and a manageable reading experience. With clear picture/text correspondence, leveled Reading Power books put the reader in charge. Now readers have the power to get the information they want and the skills they need in a user-friendly format.